I Love Learning Book Series
The Alphabet

Avant-garde Books
Children's Corner
Post Office Box 566
Mableton, Georgia 30126
www.avantgardebooks.net

I Love Learning Book Series
The Alphabet

Copyright © 2017 by Avant-garde Books, LLC
All rights reserved.

Cover and Illustrations by Suzanne Horwitz
All rights reserved.

ISBN: 978-1-946753-14-4

"Tell me and I forget. Teach me and I remember. Involve me and I learn."—Benjamin Franklin

Aa

ants

Bb

a <u>b</u>oy with <u>b</u>ooks

Cc

a <u>c</u>up of tea

Dd

three dogs

Ee

elephants

Ff

three frogs

Gg

a girl with an orange zebra

Hh

hats

Ii

an igloo

Jj

a jacket

Kk

kites

Ll

lotion

Mm

money

Nn

necklaces

Oo

an _o_ct_o_pus

Pp

parrots

Qq

a queen

Rr

red roses

Ss

the <u>s</u>un

Tt

ten toes

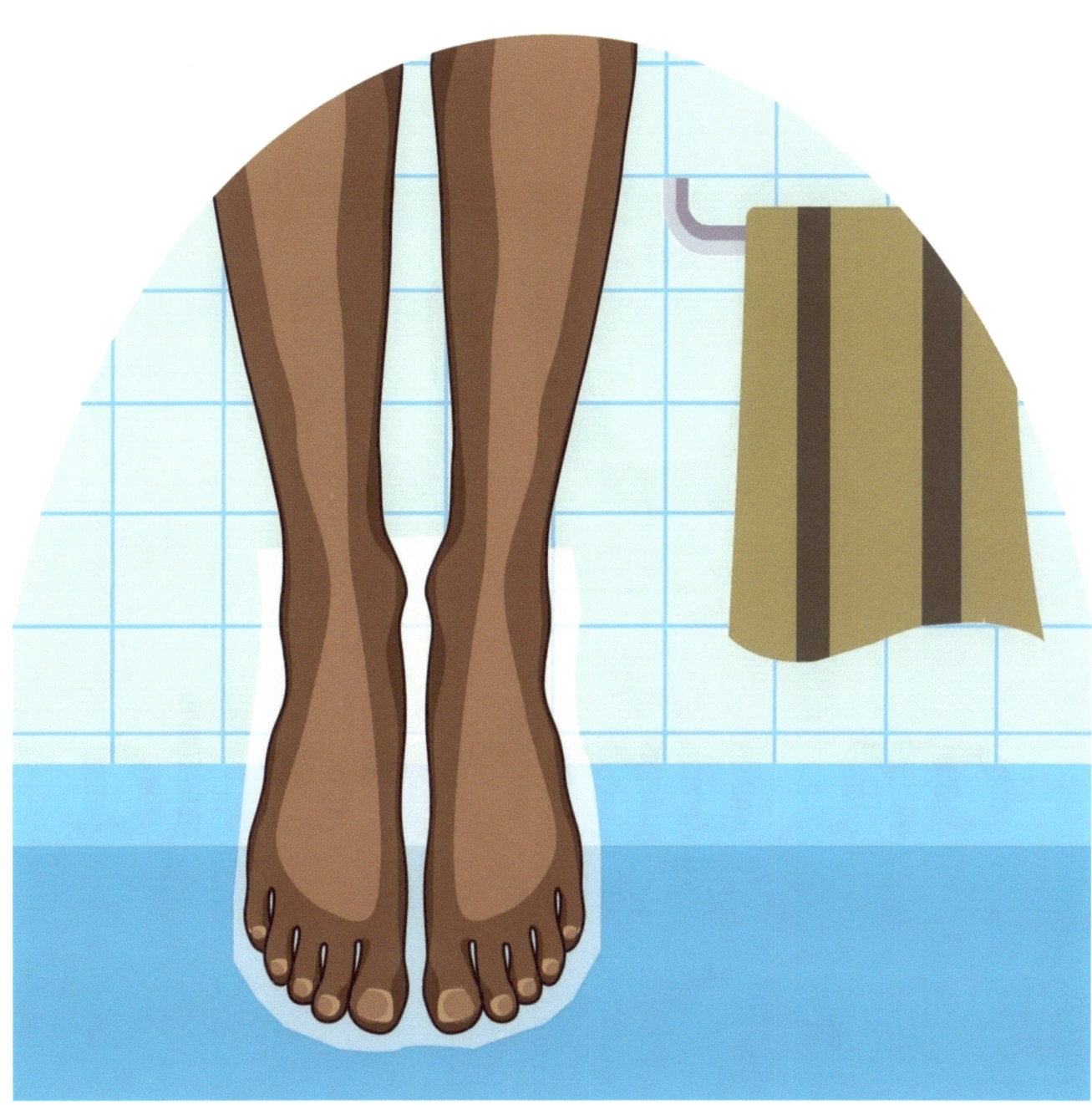

Uu

an umbrella

Vv

five vases

Ww

a <u>w</u>rist<u>w</u>atch

Xx

a xylophone

Yy

a yo-yo

Zz

four zebras

THANK YOU for your purchase!

For bulk orders, please contact us at avantgardebooks@gmail.com.

Connect with Avant-garde Books!

Facebook: @avantgardebooks100

Twitter: @Avant_GardeBks

Instagram: @avantgardebooks

Website: www.avantgardebooks.net